A CLEAN SEA: THE RACHEL CARSON STORY

A Biography for Young Children

Carol Hilgartner Schlank
and
Barbara Metzger

Illustrations:
David A. Katz

Editing:
Judith Love Cohen

Cascade
Pass, Inc.

Text Copyright © 1994 by Carol Hilgartner Schlank & Barbara Metzger
Illustrations Copyright © 1994 by Cascade Pass, Inc.
Published and designed by Cascade Pass, Inc., Suite 235, 10734 Jefferson Blvd.
Culver City CA 90230-4969
Printed by Gemini Graphics, Marina Del Rey, CA

First Edition 1994
A Clean Sea: The Rachel Carson Story was written by Carol Hilgartner Schlank and Barbara Metzger, designed and illustrated by David Katz, and edited by Judith Love Cohen.

This book is one of a series that emphasizes the environment and the value of preserving it by depicting real people who provide inspirational role models.

Library of Congress Cataloging-in-Publication Data

Schlank, Carol Hilgartner.
    A clean sea : the Rachel Carson story : a biography for young children / Carol Hilgartner Schlank and Barbara Metzger : illustrations, David A. Katz .
      p. cm.
   ISBN 1-880599-16-3 : $6.00
   1. Carson, Rachel, 1907-1964--Juvenile literature. 2. Biologists--United States--Biography--Juvenile literature.
 3. Environmentalists--United States--Biography--Juvenile literature.
[1. Carson, Rachel, 1907-1964. 2. Biologists.
3. Environmentalists. 4. Women--Biography.] I. Metzger, Barbara . II. Katz, David A. (David Arthur), 1949- ill. III. Title.
QH31.C33S34   1994
574'.092--dc20
[B]

94-45571

CIP

AC

Introduction by Judith Love Cohen

Rachel Carson, a marine biologist, was the world's first "environmentalist." In her book, *The Silent Spring,* she first warned the people of this planet that the pesticides we were using to increase agricultural yield were doing irreparable damage to the eco-system. That was in the 1960's!

Today, everyone has heard of "the environment" and pollution and toxic waste. It is particularly important that our youngest generation, who will inherit this environment, be educated so that they can participate in the movement to save their present and future home.

This series is dedicated to our planet Earth and to the individuals whose efforts have protected its resources: the oceans, the rainforests, the deserts.. all those special environments that are shared by varieties of animals and plants. This first book in that series celebrates the unique ocean and the importance of conserving ocean life, keeping ocean waters clean and wholesome and protecting ocean life from growing extinct. We do this by recounting the life and work of a very special woman, Rachel Carson, and how she first responded to a danger that no one else had yet seen.

Many years ago on a warm spring day, Rachel Carson was born. Her parents and her older brother and sister were glad to have a new baby in the family. Since her brother and sister were so much older than Rachel, they helped care for her. Rachel got lots of attention!

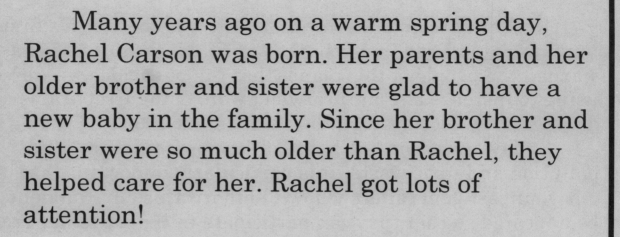

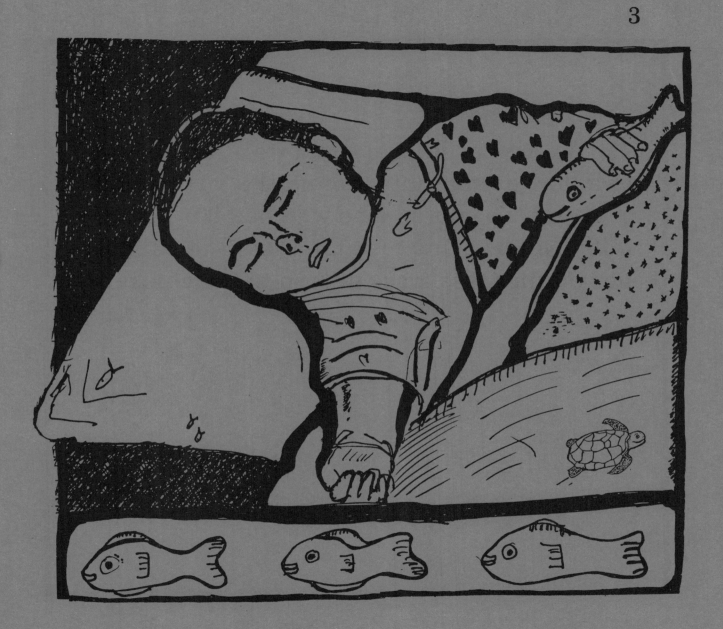

  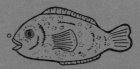

As soon as Rachel could walk, she began to follow her parents around the farm while they did the chores. She watched her father milk the cows and feed the pigs. She helped her mother toss cracked corn to the chickens.

Since her mother loved nature, she often took Rachel on walks in the woods near their house. Rachel's mother was delighted to see how interested Rachel was in living things. They spent hours together watching fish swim in the streams, butterflies drink nectar from wild flowers, and birds build nests in the woods. Rachel quickly learned the names and habits of the birds and animals.

When Rachel was six years old, her mother took her into town to school. Rachel was excited to be going to school like her big brother and sister. She loved to read and learn new things. She especially loved to read about the ocean and to listen to the sound of the sea in her mother's large conch shell. She dreamed of the day when she would finally see and hear the ocean.

After school, Rachel could hardly wait to explore the woods and fields near her home. She spent hours studying whatever she saw--from the spider spinning her web to the deer drinking from the stream. She walked in the woods in spring, summer, fall and winter watching how this small world changed with the seasons.

In the evenings, after the dishes were done, Rachel and her family would often gather around the piano and sing. Some evenings Rachel's mother would read aloud to everyone. Other times Rachel would settle down with her own books and magazines. Her favorite magazine was called *St. Nicholas*. This magazine even printed some stories written by children!

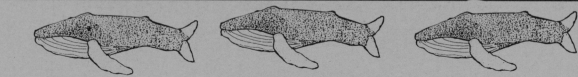

When Rachel was ten years old, she decided to write a story of her own. It was a story about a war hero her brother had known in the army. When she finished, she mailed her story to *St. Nicholas*.

She waited and waited, eagerly looking for it in each *St. Nicholas* magazine that came to her house. But she didn't find it.

"I guess it's not good enough, Mother," Rachel said sadly.

Then one day, a letter came addressed to Rachel. She tore it open.

"Mother!" she shouted. "*St. Nicholas* chose my story! And guess what? They are paying me ten dollars!" Rachel smiled proudly. Her mother smiled too. "When I grow up, " Rachel told her mother, "I am going to be an author."

When Rachel finished high school, she wanted to go away to college. Her parents did not have much money, but they scrimped and saved for her to go. Because Rachel was a good student, she won an award of one hundred dollars that also helped pay her college bills.

COLLEGE WAS THE BEGINING OF RACHEL'S NEW LIFE. SHE LOVED BOOKS!

After years of hard work, Rachel Carson became a marine biologist and studied living things in the ocean. At last she could live and work by the ocean she had longed to see when she was a child.

RACHEL CARSON STUDIED LIVING THINGS IN THE OCEAN.

At a time when almost all scientists were men, Rachel did not mind being the only woman scientist at her job. She liked wading in tide pools and walking along the ocean shores. Once she put on a diving suit and went deep into the ocean to look at the living things she could not see from a boat. She liked her work as a marine biologist, especially writing radio programs about the ocean.

At home, in the evenings, Rachel Carson began to write books. Her first book was called *Under the Sea-Wind*, and told the life stories of a mackerel, two shore birds, and an eel. After this book was published, she wrote more books about life in and near the sea. Because so many people bought her books, Rachel Carson had enough money to leave her job and spend all her time writing. Her dream of being an author had come true!

At this time, Rachel Carson became worried about reports that birds and other animals were dying from poison sprays. These sprays were used to kill insects that ate plants and crops, but they were also killing birds and other animals. Rachel was horrified. She could imagine a world in which no birds would be alive to sing.

KEEP THE BIRDS HEALTHY!

Rachel knew she had to write a book about this terrible problem. She decided to call her book *Silent Spring* to make people realize how much they would miss the singing of the birds. Although she was sick with cancer, Rachel Carson kept writing. She was determined to finish this book. Many people read *Silent Spring* and learned about the harmful chemicals that were poisoning earth, air, water and wild life.

When the President of the United States, John F. Kennedy, read her book, he asked a group of scientists to study the problems Miss Carson had written about. These scientists agreed with Rachel Carson that the environment should be protected from dangerous poisons.

Soon after the success of *Silent Spring*, Rachel Carson died. The world had lost a courageous woman, one of the first scientists to write about saving the environment. Rachel Carson's books continue to help people understand nature and realize how important it is to take care of the earth we share with all living things.

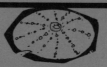
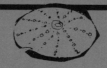

A CLEAN SEA: THE RACHEL CARSON STORY

SCIENCE LESSON PLAN 1 - TIDE POOL

PURPOSE: To familiarize children with the kind of life Rachel Carson found in the tide pools she explored.

MATERIALS: Real shells, rocks and stones, sand, driftwood, barnacles, sea plants, etc.; a water table, a small wading pool, or a baby sized tub; water and salt.

PROCEDURES: Together with the children, make a pretend tide pool using the salt water, the tub or pool and add all the other ingredients.

Have the children name and categorize the things in their tide pool

CONCLUSIONS: What are the differences between a living tide pool and a pretend tide pool?

How is a real tide pool made? Do real tide pools change?

Which things in the tide pool were once alive?

How do the objects in the tide pool feel to your touch?

SCIENCE LESSON PLAN 2 - LOOKING CLOSELY

PURPOSE: To encourage children to observe more closely and build their awareness of an ocean environment.

MATERIALS: Magnifying glasses and, if possible, a magnifying glass stand; objects from the ocean environment: fish skeleton, sponge, starfish, shells, sand, rocks, barnacles, bird feathers, seaweed, etc..

PROCEDURES: Place objects on a table and let children examine them with the magnifying glasses.

Have children name the objects and describe what they observe.

CONCLUSIONS: How do the objects look different when they are observed through the magnifying glass?

What do you notice about the object when you study it closely?

SCIENCE LESSON PLAN 3 - WHAT IS IN THE WATER?

PURPOSE: To show children that life exists even when we can't see it with the naked eye.

MATERIALS: A microscope and blank slides; a pail of ocean (or pond) water; other objects such as sand, bird feather, small sliver of driftwood, seeds, an insect, etc.

PROCEDURES: Place one of the objects under the microscope.

Have the children look and comment on what they see.

Repeat by putting a large drop of ocean or pond water on the slide and putting it under the microscope.

CONCLUSIONS: What can you see with/without the microscope?

Is there life in the water even when you can't see it?

SCIENCE LESSON PLAN 4 - OCEAN FISHING GAME

PURPOSE: To familiarize children with the variety and names of living things in an ocean habitat

MATERIALS: Pictures of various ocean habitat life forms; glue; tagboard; clear contact paper; paper clips; poles; magnets; string. Pictures might include: fish, eels, crustaceans such as shrimp, crabs, and lobsters; mammals such as sea otters, whales, dolphins, sea lions, harbor seals, and walruses; echinoderms such as starfish and sea urchins; mollusks such as snails, clams, scallops, oysters, octopi and squid; reptiles such as sea turtles and sea snakes;

PROCEDURES: Prepare the "fish" by gluing the pictures on the tagboard, covering the pictures with clear contact paper and attaching one or more paper clips to each card. Prepare the "fishing poles" by attaching one end of the string to the poles (glue, tape, staples) and a small magnet to the other end of the string (tie the string around the magnet).

Designate an area on the floor to be the "ocean" and put pictures with paper clips in this space. Have the children fish with their magnet poles, and "catch" creatures of the sea.

When a creature is "caught", have the child name and categorize their creature. They can then put the creature back in the "ocean".

CONCLUSIONS: What might you see if you lived near the ocean?

Which creatures are bigger/smaller than you are?

Which creatures spend time on land as well as in the ocean?

Which creatures lay eggs, which bear young?

Which creatures have shells?

Which creatures swim/crawl?

If you were really fishing, could you catch this creature?

SCIENCE LESSON PLAN 5 - MAKING A BOOK ABOUT THE ENVIRONMENT?

PURPOSE: To encourage children to express their interests and concerns as they relate to the environment just as Rachel Carson did.

MATERIALS: Markers, crayons, pictures of wildlife, glue, pages for a book, stapler to "bind" the book.

PROCEDURES: Have each child decide what topic to write about. Suggested topics might be ways to save the environment, a day at the ocean, or a favorite wild animal

Have the children write their story or dictate the words to an adult.

Have the children illustrate the story with their own drawings or with pictures from magazines..

SUGGESTED SUPPLEMENTARY ACTIVITIES

TRIPS: An aquarium, an arboretum, a bird sanctuary, a park, a nature preserve, a pond or brook

Have the children examine plants and animals and record their observations.

RESOURCES: Books about the environment, tapes of sounds of the ocean, bird songs, babbling brooks.

GUESTS: An environmentalist, a marine biologist, a zoologist, an ornithologist , a botanist

Invite one of these to visit your class.

About the Authors:

Carol Hilgartner Schlank and Barbara Metzger are long time early childhood experts who have worked for many years in Rochester, New York on behalf of young children. Carol has degrees from Vassar College and Nazareth College. Barbara attended St. Lawrence University and holds degrees from the University of Rochester. Ms. Schlank and Ms. Metzger have previously co-authored two books: *Martin Luther King, Jr. :A Biography for Young Children,* and *Elizabeth Cady Stanton: A Biography for Young Children.*

About the Illustrator:

David Arthur Katz received his training in art education and holds a master's degree from the University of South Florida. He is a credentialed teacher in the Los Angeles Unified School District. His involvement in the arts has included animation, illustration, and play-, poetry- and song-writing.

About the Editor:

Judith Love Cohen is a Registered Professional Electrical Engineer with bachelor's and master's degrees in engineering from the University of Southern California and University of California at Los Angeles. She has written plays, screenplays, and newspaper articles in addition to her series of children's books that began with *You Can Be a Woman Engineer.*

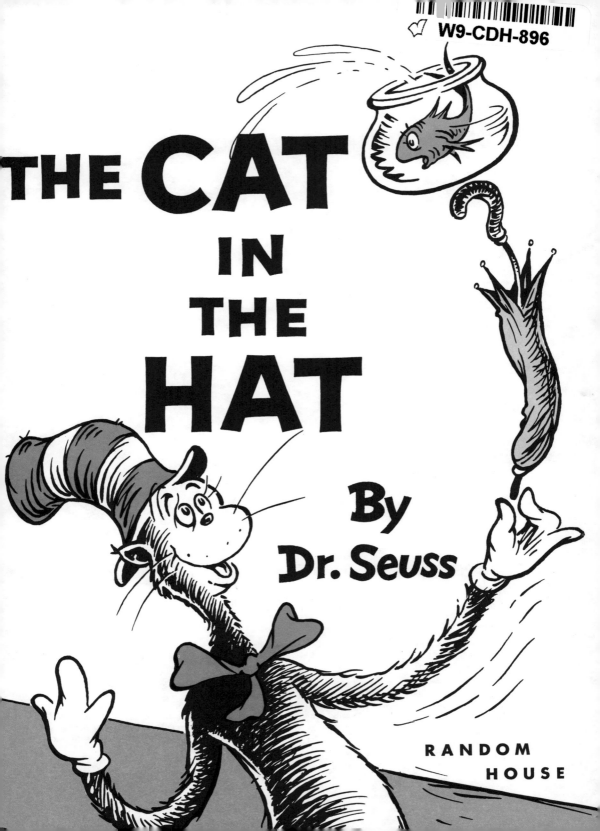

THE CAT IN THE HAT

By Dr. Seuss

RANDOM HOUSE

This title was originally catalogued by the Library of Congress as follows: Seuss, Dr. The cat in the hat, by Dr. Seuss [pseud.] Boston, Houghton Mifflin [1957] 61 p. illus. 24 cm. I. Title. PZ8.3.G276Cat 56-5470 ISBN 0-394-80001-X ISBN 0-394-90001-4

The sun did not shine.

It was too wet to play.

So we sat in the house

All that cold, cold, wet day.

1

I sat there with Sally.

We sat there, we two.

And I said, "How I wish

We had something to do!"

Too wet to go out

And too cold to play ball.

So we sat in the house.

We did nothing at all.

2

So all we could do was to
Sit!
   Sit!
      Sit!
         Sit!
And we did not like it.
Not one little bit.

And then

Something went BUMP!

How that bump made us jump!

5

We looked!

Then we saw him step in on the mat!

We looked!

And we saw him!

The Cat in the Hat!

And he said to us,

"Why do you sit there like that?"

6

"I know it is wet

And the sun is not sunny.

But we can have

Lots of good fun that is funny!"

7

"I know some good games we could play,"

Said the cat.

"I know some new tricks,"

Said the Cat in the Hat.

"A lot of good tricks.

I will show them to you.

Your mother

Will not mind at all if I do."

Then Sally and I

Did not know what to say.

Our mother was out of the house

For the day.

8

But our fish said, "No! No!
Make that cat go away!
Tell that Cat in the Hat
You do NOT want to play.
He should not be here.
He should not be about.
He should not be here
When your mother is out!"

11

"Now! Now! Have no fear.
Have no fear!" said the cat.
"My tricks are not bad,"
Said the Cat in the Hat.
"Why, we can have
Lots of good fun, if you wish,
With a game that I call
Up-up-up with a fish!"

12

"Put me down!" said the fish.

"This is no fun at all!

Put me down!" said the fish.

"I do NOT wish to fall!"

13

"Have no fear!" said the cat.

"I will not let you fall.

I will hold you up high

As I stand on a ball.

With a book on one hand!

And a cup on my hat!

But that is not ALL I can do!"

Said the cat . . .

14

"Look at me!

Look at me now!" said the cat.

"With a cup and a cake

On the top of my hat!

I can hold up two books!

I can hold up the fish!

And a little toy ship!

And some milk on a dish!

And look!

I can hop up and down on the ball!

But that is not all!

Oh, no.

That is not all . . .

"Look at me!

Look at me!

Look at me NOW!

It is fun to have fun

But you have to know how.

I can hold up the cup

And the milk and the cake!

I can hold up these books!

And the fish on a rake!

I can hold the toy ship

And a little toy man!

And look! With my tail

I can hold a red fan!

I can fan with the fan

As I hop on the ball!

But that is not all.

Oh, no.

That is not all. . . ."

That is what the cat said . . .

Then he fell on his head!

He came down with a bump

From up there on the ball.

And Sally and I,

We saw ALL the things fall!

21

And our fish came down, too.

He fell into a pot!

He said, "Do I like this?

Oh, no! I do not.

This is not a good game,"

Said our fish as he lit.

"No, I do not like it,

Not one little bit!"

22

"Now look what you did!"

Said the fish to the cat.

"Now look at this house!

Look at this! Look at that!

You sank our toy ship,

Sank it deep in the cake.

You shook up our house

And you bent our new rake.

You SHOULD NOT be here

When our mother is not.

You get out of this house!"

Said the fish in the pot.

"But I like to be here.

Oh, I like it a lot!"

Said the Cat in the Hat

To the fish in the pot.

"I will NOT go away.

I do NOT wish to go!

And so," said the Cat in the Hat,

"So

  so

    so . . .

I will show you

Another good game that I know!"

And then he ran out.

And, then, fast as a fox,

The Cat in the Hat

Came back in with a box.

A big red wood box.

It was shut with a hook.

"Now look at this trick,"

Said the cat.

"Take a look!"

Then he got up on top
With a tip of his hat.
"I call this game FUN-IN-A-BOX,"
Said the cat.
"In this box are two things
I will show to you now.
You will like these two things,"
Said the cat with a bow.

31

"I will pick up the hook.

You will see something new.

Two things. And I call them

Thing One and Thing Two.

These Things will not bite you.

They want to have fun."

Then, out of the box

Came Thing Two and Thing One!

And they ran to us fast.

They said, "How do you do?

Would you like to shake hands

With Thing One and Thing Two?"

33

And Sally and I

Did not know what to do.

So we had to shake hands

With Thing One and Thing Two.

We shook their two hands.

But our fish said, "No! No!

Those Things should not be

In this house! Make them go!

34

"They should not be here
When your mother is not!
Put them out!   Put them out!"
Said the fish in the pot.

35

"Have no fear, little fish,"
Said the Cat in the Hat.
"These Things are good Things."
And he gave them a pat.
"They are tame. Oh, so tame!
They have come here to play.
They will give you some fun
On this wet, wet, wet day."

"Now, here is a game that they like,"
Said the cat.
"They like to fly kites,"
Said the Cat in the Hat.

38

"No! Not in the house!"
Said the fish in the pot.
"They should not fly kites
In a house! They should not.
Oh, the things they will bump!
Oh, the things they will hit!
Oh, I do not like it!
Not one little bit!"

39

Then Sally and I

Saw them run down the hall.

We saw those two Things

Bump their kites on the wall!

Bump! Thump! Thump! Bump!

Down the wall in the hall.

40

Thing Two and Thing One!

They ran up! They ran down!

On the string of one kite

We saw Mother's new gown!

Her gown with the dots

That are pink, white and red.

Then we saw one kite bump

On the head of her bed!

42

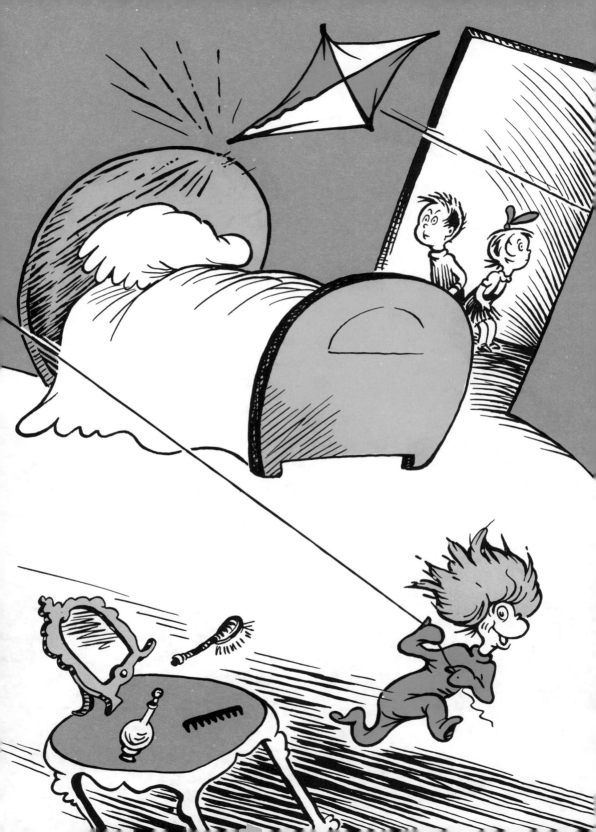

Then those Things ran about

With big bumps, jumps and kicks

And with hops and big thumps

And all kinds of bad tricks.

And I said,

"I do NOT like the way that they play!

If Mother could see this,

Oh, what would she say!"

45

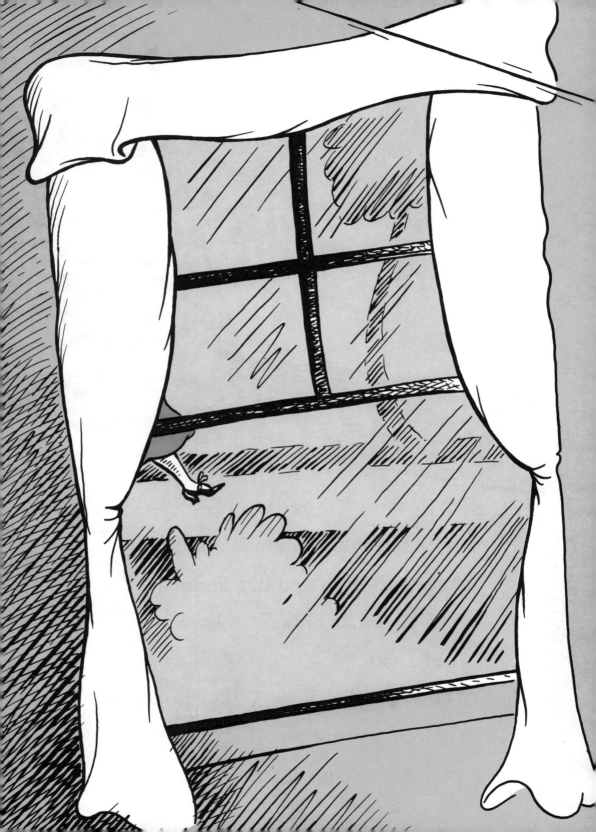

Then our fish said, "LOOK! LOOK!"

And our fish shook with fear.

"Your mother is on her way home!

Do you hear?

Oh, what will she do to us?

What will she say?

Oh, she will not like it

To find us this way!"

47

"So, DO something! Fast!" said the fish.

"Do you hear!

I saw her. Your mother!

Your mother is near!

So, as fast as you can,

Think of something to do!

You will have to get rid of

Thing One and Thing Two!"

So, as fast as I could,

I went after my net.

And I said, "With my net

I can get them I bet.

I bet, with my net,

I can get those Things yet!"

Then I let down my net.

It came down with a PLOP!

And I had them! At last!

Those two Things had to stop.

Then I said to the cat,

"Now you do as I say.

You pack up those Things

And you take them away!"

PLOP

"Oh dear!" said the cat.

"You did not like our game . . .

Oh dear.

What a shame!

What a shame!

What a shame!"

53

Then he shut up the Things
In the box with the hook.
And the cat went away
With a sad kind of look.

"That is good," said the fish.

"He has gone away.   Yes.

But your mother will come.

She will find this big mess!

And this mess is so big

And so deep and so tall,

We can not pick it up.

There is no way at all!"

55

And THEN!

Who was back in the house?

Why, the cat!

"Have no fear of this mess,"

Said the Cat in the Hat.

"I always pick up all my playthings

And so . . .

I will show you another

Good trick that I know!"

57

Then we saw him pick up

All the things that were down.

He picked up the cake,

And the rake, and the gown,

And the milk, and the strings,

And the books, and the dish,

And the fan, and the cup,

And the ship, and the fish.

And he put them away.

Then he said, "That is that."

And then he was gone

With a tip of his hat.

Then our mother came in
And she said to us two,
"Did you have any fun?
Tell me. What did you do?"

And Sally and I did not know
What to say.
Should we tell her
The things that went on there that day?

Should we tell her about it?

Now, what SHOULD we do?

Well . . .

What would YOU do

If your mother asked YOU?